TABLE

1 – Your New Life Now – pg. 1

2 – You have Access to God – pg. 5

3 – Steps To Growing In Grace – pg. 9

4 – Study The Word Daily – pg. 11

5 – Spend Time In Prayer – pg. 14

6 – Join A Church – pg. 17

7 – Get Involved – pg. 19

Share your New Faith – pg. 24

About The Authors – pg. 25

STEPS TO GROWING IN GRACE!

The Renewing of Your Mind

ROSEMARY & CHARLES OKOLO

Unless otherwise indicated, all scripture quotations are taken from the Holy Bible, Amplified Version.

STEPS TO GROWING IN GRACE!

The renewing of your mind

ISBN- 13: 978-1534692855

ISBN- 10: 1534692851

Copyright © 2016 Rosemary & Charles Okolo

Published by Rosemary Okolo Publications

In partnership with Infallible Word Ministries

United Kingdom

www.rosemaryokolo.org

www.infallibleword.org.uk

All rights reserved under International Copyright Law. No part of this book may be reproduced, stored in a retrieval system, or transmitted by any means without the prior written permission of the Authors

Chapter One

YOUR NEW LIFE NOW!

Congratulations! Now you are born again. It's the most important decision anyone could ever make in their lives! You have made it, well done. Welcome to the family and into your new reality. Welcome to the family of GOD! We rejoice with you and the host of heaven rejoices with you as well.

"In the same way, I tell you, there is rejoicing in the presence of the angels of God over one sinner who repents." Luke 15: 10

We would like to share with you some truth from God's Word concerning your new birth in Christ Jesus. You see, the Bible clearly says that we were created in the image of God.

"Then God said, "Let us make mankind in our image, in our likeness, so that they may rule over the fish in the sea and the birds in the sky, over the livestock and all the wild animals, and over all the creatures that move along the ground. So God created mankind in His own image, in the image of God He created them; male and female He created them." Genesis 1:26-27

We are a spirit first, we have a soul which consists of our intellect, will and emotions and we live in a physical body. The real you is your spirit. That's the part of you that was created in the image of God, that got born again and looks like God.

When we die, our body will return to dust in the ground but we live on, our spirit, the real us lives on, and so when you get born again, that is when you received Jesus into your life, it's your spirit that was regenerated, that got born again and not your physical body.

And so, we have to continually renew our minds through the Word of God by bringing our body under subjection to God's Word, so we can live in our physical body but be ruled and guided by our born again spirit. The Bible says,

"May God Himself, the God of peace, sanctify you through and through. May your whole spirit, soul and body be kept blameless at the coming of our Lord Jesus Christ." 1 Thessalonians 5:23

YOU ARE SPIRIT, SOUL AND BODY

You are a spirit with a soul, living in a body. Your spirit, soul and body is what makes up our personality. Our body is what holds up our spirit.

It is the house of our spirit. Our spirit dwells in our body. Our body is what we all see, feel and touch.

"Therefore, I urge you, brothers and sisters, in view of God's mercy, to offer your bodies as a living sacrifice, holy and pleasing to God—this is your true and proper worship." Romans 12:1

Our soul consists of our mind, will and emotions. We can only grow spiritually and prosper only to the degree that our soul prospers and knows God.

We therefore have the responsibility to renew our mind, will and emotions (Our soul) by the Word of God.

"Dear friend, I pray that you may enjoy good health and that all may go well with you, even as your soul is getting along well." 3 John 1:2

You see, when a person dies, the spirit of that person still lives on, even though the flesh is dead. The body gets buried or cremated but the person lives on, in the spirit realm.

They have their senses and are conscious of everything around them. Please read the story in the Book of Luke Chapter 16. About two men who died named Lazarus and the rich man.

Their spirit still lived on and they could recognise each other and even remembered their lives back on earth when they were alive in their physical bodies.

Therefore, when you get born again, it's your spirit man that gets born again. The real you! It is through our spirit that we can truly have fellowship and communion with God.

Chapter Two

YOU HAVE FULL ACCESS TO GOD!

"Therefore, brothers and sisters, since we have confidence to enter the Most Holy Place by the blood of Jesus," Hebrews 10:19

Jesus took our sins upon Himself and died for us so we can have a great life and be able to stand and come before God freely and without shame, guilt or inferiority. He paid the price for us! You and me now have peace with God! The Bible says that,

"Therefore, since we have been justified through faith, we have peace with God through our Lord Jesus Christ," Romans 5:1

Christ Jesus has made us the righteousness of God! We can now stand before Almighty God as though we have never sinned before. Yes, absolutely! In God's sight, we are not guilty before Him. We stand sinless before Him!

"God made him who had no sin to be sin for us, so that in him we might become the righteousness of God." 2 Corinthians 5:21

God is no more holding our sins against us. Jesus made this possible for us and now that you are born again, you are a brand new creature, you are the righteousness of God in Christ Jesus and you stand blameless before God.

"That God was reconciling the world to Himself in Christ, not counting people's sins against them. And He has committed to us the message of reconciliation." 2 Corinthians 5:19

Don't think low of yourself like you used to before you got born again. Forget the past, forget all your past life and how you had lived and embrace this new life you now have in Christ Jesus.

"…But you were washed, you were sanctified, you were justified in the name of the Lord Jesus Christ and by the Spirit of our God." 1 Corinthians 6:11

You have to renew your mind to this truth so you can live a life of victory. For by renewing your mind through God's Word, you will begin to see yourself and see things through God's eyes and through His ways, from His point of view – His Word!

You have full access to God through the Holy Spirit. You can go before God with boldness and confidence. You have the Holy Spirit in you. The Holy Spirit is a person, not some kind of force. He is the third person of the Trinity.

He is our best teacher and God promised us in His Word that, He will send His Spirit to dwell in us so His Spirit will be our Helper, Teacher and so much more. He will teach us God's Word, speak to us and guide us always and forever!

"But the Advocate, the Holy Spirit, whom the Father will send in my name, will teach you all things and will remind you of everything I have said to you." John 14:26

"But when He, the Spirit of Truth, comes, He will guide you into all the truth [full and complete truth]. For He will not speak on His own initiative, but He will speak whatever He hears [from the Father—the message regarding the Son], and He will disclose to you what is to come [in the future]." John 16:13

He has always been in existence before the foundations of the earth and before time existed. He is the One who accomplishes whatever words the Father speaks. He is the spirit of love and He empowers us to become all that God has called us to be.

He energizes us and makes us more effective, by His power in us. The "Dunamis" power in us, that divine power and ability to bring about changes to our lives and circumstances. He teaches us the Word of God. He is always for us and with us and He anoints us to do what God called us to do!

"But you will receive power when the Holy Spirit comes on you; and you will be my witnesses in Jerusalem, and in all Judea and Samaria, and to the ends of the earth." Acts 1:8

"The Spirit Himself testifies *and* confirms together with our spirit [assuring us] that we [believers] are children of God." Romans 8:16

He bears witness with our spirit that we are the children of God and partakers of Christ riches and inheritance. Get into relationship with Him. Recognise and acknowledge His presence in your live.

Listen to Him and speak with Him. As you take time to pray and study God's Word daily, you will begin to know Him more. He loves you and He is there to help you, guide you and direct you.

"And I will ask the Father, and He will give you another Helper (Comforter, Advocate, Intercessor, Counsellor, Strengthener, Standby), to be with you forever the Spirit of Truth, whom the world cannot receive [and take to its heart] because it does not see Him or know Him, *but* you know Him because He (the Holy Spirit) remains with you *continually* and will be in you." John 14:16-17

Chapter Three

STEPS TO GROWING IN GRACE

Now that you are born again, you are a child of God. He loves you and wants the very best for you. Now, you have a relationship with Him because, He is your Heavenly Father. Friend, it is not enough to only have a relationship with Him. Get into fellowship!

Go beyond relationship and into having fellowship with Him. Fellowship is getting to know Him and understand Him on a more personal level. You see, when you fellowship with God, you get to know Him better and understand His Will and purpose for your life.

Some people hear about God, sing about God, and read about God and that's fine but that's not enough. Not everyone fellowships with Him, and knowing Him on a personal level and to be personally known by Him.

Fellowshipping with Him is spending time with Him, speaking to Him and with Him and knowing His voice. God loves us and desires and longs to have fellowship with us, with you.

When you love somebody so much, you want to fellowship with them, you want to always be in their presence and talk, chat and enjoy each other's presence. That's exactly what God wants with you.

He wants to hear you talk with Him, share your thoughts with Him, your dreams and desires and He wants to see that you are happy and accomplish all that will bring you joy and give Him Glory.

There are a number of ways that you can have fellowship with God and grow in grace. Let's look at some of the important ones that will help you to grow in grace in your new birth and relationship with your Heavenly Father, as you take the steps to grow in grace.

Chapter Four

STUDY THE WORD DAILY

One of the best ways you can get into fellowship with God and understand His Will and purpose for your life, grow in grace and become your very best you is to spend time in the Word of God daily.

Take out time to study the Bible. You see, personal experiences and testimonies of other believers can encourage us and help us to know more about God and His goodness, faithfulness etc. The Word of God is the best success book in the world!

"This Book of the Law shall not depart from your mouth, but you shall read [and meditate on] it day and night, so that you may be careful to do [everything] in accordance with all that is written in it; for then you will make your way prosperous, and then you will be successful." Joshua 1:8

The Word of God will teach you how to become successful and accomplish your God given dreams and prosper in it! The Word of God will teach you how to live a good life and a life that is pleasing to God and how to remain successful.

As you spend time in God's Word, you are spending time in His Presence and fellowshipping with Him.

"In the beginning [before all-time] was the Word (Christ), and the Word was with God, and the Word was God Himself." John 1:1

God loves you so much, and as you spend time in His Word, you will begin to increase in the knowledge of Him. You will begin to know more about Him, about His ways, his plans for you and you will begin to know more about who you truly are in Him.

You will begin to know true success and begin to know His great and awesome love for you!

"I have loved you just as the Father has loved Me; remain in My love [and do not doubt My love for you]. If you keep My commandments *and* obey My teaching, you will remain in My love, just as I have kept My Father's commandments and remain in His love." John 15:9-10

Set out a time and probably a place where you can relax and quietly spend valuable time in His presence, before Him, in His Word. It maybe for 10 minutes, 15, 20 minutes or more, and it may be less but it doesn't matter.

Start wherever you can and as you do it consistently, you will begin to get enough time and enjoy the time you spend with His Word, regardless of how little it may seem.

Friend, develop the discipline of spending time in God's Word. You will never remain the same again. God will give you the grace to create the time as you faithfully seek after Him.

It may be helpful to start reading the New Testament and you could start reading the Bible from the Book of Matthew or you could start with the Book of John.

One or two Chapters a day, a few verses or more, it really doesn't matter how you start. As you continue to read the Bible, you will begin to love to study God's Word!

Chapter Five

SPEND TIME IN PRAYER

"For God did not give us a spirit of timidity *or* cowardice *or* fear, but [He has given us a spirit] of power and of love and of sound judgment *and* personal discipline [abilities that result in a calm, well-balanced mind and self-control]." 2 Timothy 1:7

Now that you are born again, you can come into the presence of God without fear, shame, guilt or inferiority by the blood of His Son Jesus because of what He has done for you. Prayer is one of the sweetest form of communication to God. Praying to God is simply acknowledging He is with you, and knowing that He loves you and hears your prayer.

It is like talking to your dad or someone you truly love and respect. When we pray to your Heavenly Father (God), the Bible says that, we should pray in the name of Jesus, His Son. So we come into His Presence and pray to Him through His Son, Jesus.

He has promised us that, when we ask anything in His Name, according to His Will,

He will do it. He will answer our prayer, so that He, will be glorified through you.

"And I will do whatever you ask in my name, so that the Father may be glorified in the Son. You may ask me for anything in my name, and I will do it." John 14:13-14

Take out time to speak to Him, praise Him and worship Him. Stay quiet before Him as well, so you can hear Him speak back to you. He always loves to hear us speak with Him and He loves to speak back to us. Enjoy His presence and be expectant.

Expect that He will speak to you and give you direction for your life. God truly loves you more than anyone could ever love you and He cares about you. You can speak to Him anywhere and anytime.

However, it's a good idea to pick out a time and place when you can go into His presence with a notebook or note pad and a pen and speak, pray to Him and expect to hear Him speak back to you, and then you can write down what He said to you, the scripture He put in your heart to read etc.

You could do these at the time you set aside to study His Word or before. You see, as you intentionally make out time to spend with God your Heavenly Father, you are acknowledging His very presence in your life!

Nothing is too insignificant to tell God about and nothing is too big to tell God about. Always be open to Him. Remember, He already knows you, your thoughts and all but He loves it when you still speak to Him about them. He cares about you and He is never too busy to listen to you!

Chapter Six

JOIN A WORD CHURCH

Your New Family

Now that you are born again, you belong to a great family of believers of God, the Church. The Church is the body of Christ and Christ is the Head of the Church. Attend Church meetings or Christian gatherings that obey the Word of God regularly.

"For as the body is one and has many members, but all the members of that one body, being many, are one body, so also *is* Christ. For by one Spirit we were all baptized into one body—whether Jews or Greeks, whether slaves or free—and have all been made to drink into one Spirit. For in fact the body is not one member but many."

1 Corinthians 12:12-14 NKJV

Maybe right now, you don't have any family, but guess what? You do! You are never alone.

"Now you [collectively] are Christ's body, and individually [you are] members of it [each with his own special purpose and function]."

1 Corinthians 12:27

You now belong to a great family of God who would love and appreciate you and help you through your journey as a Christian, a believer of the Lord Jesus. Join a good Church.

A Church that believes in the Lord Jesus as Lord and Saviour. A Church that teaches and preaches the uncompromising Word of God with integrity and provides accurate Bible based teaching.

A Church that has financial integrity and a Church with a sense of family, operating in the love of God. You may ask, does such a Church exist?

Yes, friend! Such a Church does exist. Pray about it. Ask God to lead you to the right Church and He will. The Bible says that, He directs the path of the righteous. God will direct you as you seek Him with your heart.

"In all your ways know and acknowledge and recognise Him, and He will make your paths straight and smooth [removing obstacles that block your way]." Proverbs 3:6

Chapter Seven

GET INVOLVED!

Attend Regular Bible Studies at your Church and get involved! Join a House Fellowship and learn more about God and make new relationships with like-minded believers who want to know God more and growing in grace.

"Not forsaking our meeting together [as believers for worship and instruction], as is the habit of some, but encouraging *one another*; and all the more [faithfully] as you see the day [of Christ's return] approaching." Hebrews 10:25

"Iron sharpens iron; so a man sharpens the countenance of his friend [to show rage or worthy purpose]." Proverbs 27:17

Who are your friends? Get new friends who will sharpen you. It has been said that, the people you spend more of your time with will determine what kind of a person you are and most likely will grow up to be.

The right friends can be a blessing and empower you to succeed in life and the wrong ones can be a curse and empower you to fail. Good friends will motivate you to obey God and succeed in life.

Hanging out with believers at your House Fellowship, at Church, people who love God.

Honest people and people who will show you more of God from their lives and the Word of God is so very important in growing in grace.

Who are you constantly hanging out with? Are they lovers of God? Are they honest people who tell you the truth? Or are they people who just tell you what you want to hear?

Hang around people who would influence you to be a better person and be the best that you can be.

Friend, hang around believers, friends who will help you get closer to God and not pull you away from Him. Now evaluate yourself, how careful are you about your choice of friends.

How would you rate yourself as a friend? Do you measure up to the world's standards or God's standards?

Attending a study group, or House fellowship is an opportunity to grow and be a blessing to one another.

Edifying each other with your different gifting and a great place to make great godly friends and friendships.

And as you pray and worship God together, a corporate anointing is released amongst you all by the Holy Spirit.

GET BAPTISED IN THE HOLY SPIRIT

Now that you are born again, you are a Child of Almighty God. Get filled with the Holy Spirit with the evidence of speaking in tongues. This is an important part of your faith and growth in Christ Jesus. It's your covenant right to speak in tongues. And all you need to do is ask God to fill you with the Holy Spirit. He said in His Word that,

"What father among you, if his son asks for a fish, will give him a snake instead of a fish? Or if he asks for an egg, will give him a scorpion? If you, then, being evil [that is, sinful by nature], know how to give good gifts to your children, how much more will your heavenly Father give the Holy Spirit to those who ask *and* continue to ask Him!" Luke 11:11-13

All you need to do is ask God in prayer according to His Word. Believe in your heart that you will receive the gift of tongues as you ask God. Expect God to give you the utterance to speak in tongues out from your mouth.

Now pray this prayer with me:

Prayer for Baptism in the Holy Spirit

Father, thank you for the gift of tongues. You said you will give the Holy Spirit to those who ask. According to your Word in Luke 11:13, I ask you now to fill me with the Holy Spirit with the evidence of speaking out in tongues. Thank you Lord, for filling me with the Holy Spirit with the evidence of speaking out in other tongues. I believe and receive it now and do speak in tongues now in Jesus Name - Amen. Thank you Lord!

Congratulations! Now, you are filled with the Holy Spirit. Begin to thank Him for filling you with the Holy Spirit. Open your mouth now and begin to speak out in tongues. Speak those syllables you receive. Speak them out in faith. Just speak them out...yes, let it flow...

It's not going to be in your own language but a new language given to you by the Holy spirit. Speak it out using your own voice and mouth. Don't think about what is coming out of your mouth, and how it sounds. Just speak it out in faith! If you didn't get to speak it out today, it's alright.

Continue to thank God for filling you with the Holy Spirit and keep your expectations high, expecting to speak it out because you believe you are already filled.

Truth is, you received it when you asked God for it by faith. You already have it. Be bold and confident and speak whatever comes out of your mouth.

Pray consistently in tongues and as you continue, it would begin to flow smoothly from your mouth. Give God praise and stay joyful!

SHARE YOUR NEW FAITH

Tell your friends and loved ones about Jesus and what He has done for you! Tell others about your new found faith in God. Share your testimony with them and tell them about the love of God that you now know and are experiencing. Share the Good news!

Don't be shy to talk about your new found faith in Christ Jesus. God loves it when we care about other people enough to let them know about His love for them.

Jesus said, "Therefore whoever confesses Me before men, him I will also confess before My Father who is in heaven." Matthew 10:32

ABOUT THE AUTHORS

Charles and Rosemary Okolo have a passion to reach out to the lost and mentor young believers. They are the founders of Infallible Word Ministries. It's an outreach, with a mission to reach out to the lost and the hurting, share God's Word and His unconditional love to them.

Mentor young believers worldwide and teach them who they are in Christ Jesus and how to live a victorious life in their covenant rights and privileges.

They are also involved and serve in the Prison Ministries, taking every opportunity given, to encourage the inmates through the ministry of the Word of encouragement and through the Music Ministry.

They are happily married for Twenty Two Years at the time of writing this book and both live together in the United Kingdom, with their three Children serving God.

We trust that this book has been a blessing to you. Why not share your joy, testimony and prayer points with us by visiting our website.

Learn more about

Infallible Word Ministries

By visiting our website:

www.infallibleword.org.uk

www.rosemaryokolo.org

Printed in Great Britain
by Amazon